Second Edition

Jacob's Ladder

Grade

Reading Comprehension Program

Student Workbook
Nonfiction

Student Name: _____

Teacher: _____

Center for Gifted Education, William & Mary

Jacob's Ladder Reading Comprehension Program

Second Edition

Grade 3

Student Workbook Nonfiction

Contributing Editors:
Joyce VanTassel-Baska,
Tamra Stambaugh,
Kimberley L. Chandler

Contributing Authors:
Heather French,
Paula Ginsburgh,
Tamra Stambaugh,
Joyce VanTassel-Baska

William & Mary
School of Education
CENTER FOR GIFTED EDUCATION

William & Mary
School of Education
Center for Gifted Education
P.O. Box 8795
Williamsburg, VA 23187

First published in 2017 by Prufrock Press Inc.

Published in 2021 by Routledge
605 Third Avenue, New York, NY 10017
2 Park Square, Milton Park, Abingdon, Oxon OX14 4RN

Routledge is an imprint of the Taylor & Francis Group, an informa business.

ISBN: 978-1-61821-732-5

Routledge
Taylor & Francis Group
NEW YORK AND LONDON

Table of Contents

Ancient Rome

According to legend, Rome was founded by twin brothers, Romulus and Remus, in 753 B.C.E. Archaeological evidence of Ancient Rome dates to the 8th century B.C.E., somewhere between 800 B.C.E. and 701 B.C.E. (Remember, in B.C.E., the smaller the number, the more recent the date, so 701 B.C.E. is closer to modern day than 800 B.C.E.) For nearly 1,000 years, Rome was the most important, richest, most powerful city in the Western world. During this time, Rome went through several major changes.

Rome began as the Roman Kingdom. It was ruled by a succession of seven kings. Some time between 509 B.C.E. and 501 B.C.E., the last of the seven kings, Tarquin the Proud, was deposed from his throne, which means he was removed from power. With the end of Tarquin the Proud's reign, the Roman Kingdom became the Roman Republic.

The Roman Republic was governed by a senate rather than a monarch or king. The original senate consisted of 100 heads of Roman families. The senate did not have actual lawmaking powers. Rather, it made recommendations to the Plebeian Council, which received its power from the Roman people. Over time, the senate grew in number and in power. By the end of the Roman Republic, there were more than 300 members of the senate. Although they did not have the power to make laws, the senate held remarkable political power. The senate was responsible for sending and receiving ambassadors to foreign lands, appointing managers of public lands, conducting wars, and distributing public funds.

The Roman Republic came to an end when, in the middle of the first century B.C.E., three men formed the First Triumvirate (trahy-**uhm**-ver-it). These three men were Julius Caesar, Pompey the Great (**pom**-pee), and Crassus (**kras**-*uhs*). They plotted to control the Roman Republic, and their schemes led to civil war. In 44 B.C.E., Julius Caesar was assassinated, or killed, by senators who did not agree with his politics. Eventually, through a series of struggles for power, Augustus, Caesar's designated heir, gained control and became the undisputed ruler of Rome.

With the ascent of Augustus to power, the Roman Republic became the Roman Empire. The Roman Empire extended across most of Europe to the Mediterranean Sea with a population

that exceeded 50 million people. During the "Reign of Five Good Emperors" from 96–180 C.E., the Roman Empire reached its largest landmass of 2 million square miles. Eventually, the Empire became so large that it was nearly impossible for one ruler to maintain control of the entire Empire. In 293 C.E., the Emperor Diocletian (dahy-*uh*-**klee**-sh*uh*n) divided the Roman Empire into an eastern half and a western half. This division became permanent in 330 C.E. after Constantine established Constantinople as the capital of the Eastern Roman Empire. The Western Empire continued to be known as the Roman Empire. The Empire came to a dramatic end in 476 C.E. when Odoacer, a barbarian warlord, killed the last Western Emperor, Romulus Augustulus. Odoacer then made himself king of Italy. The Byzantine Empire in the east came to a less dramatic end in 1453 C.E. when the ruler of the Ottoman Empire, Mehmed II, conquered Constantinople.

ANCIENT ROME

Consequences and Implications

A3 What consequences did the Roman Empire experience because of its large size?

_____

_____

_____

What were the implications of these consequences? Justify your answer.

_____

_____

_____

Cause and Effect

A2 What caused the Roman Republic to end? Use evidence from the text to support your answer.

_____

_____

_____

_____

Sequencing

A1 In the space below, create a timeline of the major events in the history of Ancient Rome.

Creative Synthesis

D3   Choose an era from Ancient Rome—the Roman Kingdom, the Roman Republic, or the Roman Empire. Imagine you are a Roman citizen during one of these eras. Write a journal entry about what is happening in your city.

_____

_____

_____

_____

_____

_____

_____

_____

_____

Summarizing

D2   In three sentences or fewer, summarize the fall of the Roman Republic and the rise of the Roman Empire.

_____

_____

_____

_____

_____

Paraphrasing

D1   Rewrite the following statement in your own words:

"For nearly 1,000 years, Rome was the most important, richest, most powerful city in the Western world."

_____

_____

_____

_____

The Circle of Life

All animals journey through a predictable life cycle during their life-span. Most animals, except mammals that give birth to live young, begin as eggs. The female of the species lays the eggs, which begins the life cycle of a new animal. Different kinds of animals experience different life cycles. Let's compare the life cycle of amphibians (ām-fĭb'ē-ənz) and insects.

Amphibians

Amphibians, such as frogs, live their entire lives near water because they must return to the water to lay their eggs. Amphibians experience a three-stage life cycle. The stages are the egg stage, the larval stage, and the adult stage. The female amphibians lay their eggs directly in the water, thus beginning the egg stage. When the eggs hatch, the larval stage begins as tadpoles emerge with gills for breathing. As amphibians mature, they develop lungs that allow them to breathe outside of the water. They also begin growing legs and losing their tails. This process is called *metamorphosis* (met-*uh*-**mawr**-*fuh*-sis), which means a complete change in form. During metamorphosis, amphibians change from gill breathers to lung breathers and from plant eaters to meat eaters (think about a frog sitting on the side of a pond catching bugs—meat—with its long, sticky tongue). Some amphibians, such as salamanders and newts, do not undergo metamorphosis. Instead, they spend their entire lives in the larval stage. They do not develop lungs or lose their tails, and they only grow very short legs.

Insects

Winged insects and nonwinged insects experience two different life cycles. Both types of insects begin as eggs. They both have a larval stage, a pupa stage, and a metamorphosis. However, they journey through these stages in different ways.

Nonwinged Insects

Nonwinged insects have a hard outer skeleton called an *exoskeleton* that protects them. Because of this hard outer covering, these insects must grow in stages. The insects eat, grow larger, and then must periodically shed their exoskeleton through a process called *ecdysis* (**ek**-*duh*-sis). Each time the insect sheds its exoskeleton, it is bigger and more mature.

Therefore, metamorphosis—or the complete change from larva to adult insect—happens gradually over time. Scientists have named this gradual change *simple metamorphosis*.

Winged Insects

Winged insects, such as butterflies and ladybugs, experience four distinct life cycle phases. Like most other animals, they begin their lives as eggs. When they hatch, they enter the larval stage. During the larval stage, a butterfly is called a caterpillar and a ladybug is called a Ladybird beetle. The length of the larval stage varies among species, but during this stage the insects eat and grow. Eventually, the larvae are ready to enter the next stage: The larvae become pupae by encasing themselves inside a chrysalis (**kris**-*uh*-lis) or cocoon. While in the chrysalis, the winged insect undergoes a complete transformation and emerges as an adult butterfly or ladybug. The adult winged insect looks completely different than the larva. Scientists have named this complete transformation *complex metamorphosis*.

THE CIRCLE OF LIFE

Consequences and Implications

A3 What are the consequences of an amphibian or an insect reaching the final stage in the life cycle?

_____

_____

_____

_____

_____

Cause and Effect

A2 What causes a nonwinged insect to move to the next stage of simple metamorphosis?

_____

_____

_____

_____

_____

Sequencing

A1 List, in order, the following:
Stages of an amphibian's life cycle

_____

_____

_____

Stages of a winged insect's life cycle

_____

_____

_____

Creative Synthesis

D3 Write about the process of metamorphosis from the perspective of an amphibian, a nonwinged insect, or a winged insect.

_____

_____

_____

_____

_____

_____

Summarizing

D2 Describe the life cycle of nonwinged insects versus that of winged insects in three sentences or less.

_____

_____

_____

_____

_____

_____

Paraphrasing

D1 Rewrite this statement in your own words:

> "Therefore, metamorphosis—or the complete change from larva to adult insect—happens gradually over time. Scientists have named this gradual change _simple metamorphosis_."

_____

_____

_____

_____

_____

_____

_____

Geometry All Around Us

Have you ever looked around your classroom, your kitchen, or your backyard and noticed all of the geometry around you? Geometry includes all of the many shapes, lines, angles, points, quadrants, square inches, square feet, and square yards that you see every day.

Look around your classroom. How many different shapes can you find? The board at the front of the room is probably a rectangle. Perhaps the table where you sit is a circle. Maybe there is a globe somewhere in your classroom. A globe is a three-dimensional shape called a *sphere*. What about angles? How many angles do you see in your classroom? Perhaps your chair is connected to your desk. Is the seat at a 90-degree, or right, angle? Or, is it slightly tilted back at a 105- or 110-degree angle? Are the corners of the windows right angles?

Now let's think about your house. Your roof may be shaped like a triangle or perhaps a trapezoid. The walls in your house may form straight lines or they may have some angled corners. Do you know how many square feet are in your house? The architect who designed your house and the contractor who built it used geometry to determine how large each room should be, where the exterior and interior walls should go, and how much square footage the finished home should have. Can you think of another way geometry is used in the building of houses? Here's one example: An architect creates a two-dimensional drawing of a house using lines, points, and angles. The architect gives this two-dimensional drawing to the contractor who then transforms it into a three-dimensional building.

Let's think about your yard. Are there flower gardens? How do your parents know how much potting soil or mulch to buy for the flower gardens? They use geometry to figure out the areas of the different flowerbeds. Once they know the square footage of each bed, they know how much dirt or mulch is needed to fill each area. Farmers use this same technique when they are deciding how and where to plant their crops. They use geometry to calculate the area of their fields. In places as large as fields, the area often is referred to as acres. One acre is 4,840 square yards or 43,560 square feet. That's a lot of area!

Geometry also is a big part of activities we do every day. For example, when you are driving somewhere new, how do you know where to go? You might look at a map. When looking at a map, you are using geometry. Maps are made up of quadrants,

points, and lines. You use the map's key to determine in what quadrant your desired location is; then you follow the lines, or roads, until you reach your destination, which is a point on the map.

Have you ever ridden a skateboard or seen skateboarders riding on ramps? The skateboarders use geometry, even if they don't realize it, when they build their ramps. They must determine the perfect arc for the performance of their tricks. If the arc of the ramp is too steep, they will lose speed and may not make it to the top. However, if the arc of the ramp is too shallow, the skateboarders will not get enough height to perform their tricks. So, the skateboarders must design their ramps with the perfect arc to give them the right amount of speed and the right amount of height.

These are just a few examples of the many different ways geometry is used in everyday life. The next time you are walking down the street, look around you—how many examples of geometry do you see?

GEOMETRY ALL AROUND US

Generalizations

B3 Write at least three generalizations about geometry and your everyday life.

_____

_____

_____

_____

Classifications

B2 Study your list from B1. Classify the examples into categories you create. You may not have a "miscellaneous" or "other" category.

_____

_____

_____

_____

_____

_____

_____

Details

B1 Look around you. List as many examples of geometry as you can in 2 minutes. (You should have at least 25 examples.)

_____

_____

_____

_____

_____

_____

_____

_____

_____

_____

Main Idea, Theme, or Concept

C3   Main Idea: What is the main idea of "Geometry All Around Us"? Justify your answer.

_____

_____

_____

_____

_____

_____

Inference

C2   Based on the text, what inferences can you make about the use of geometry?

_____

_____

_____

_____

_____

_____

Literary Elements

C1   An architect's use of geometry might be characterized as design, and a farmer's use of geometry might be characterized as agricultural. How might a skateboarder's use of geometry be characterized? Use evidence from the text to support your answer.

_____

_____

_____

_____

_____

_____

_____

The Industrial Revolution

The Industrial Revolution began in Great Britain during the late 18th century and early 19th century. During the Revolution, manual labor was replaced by industry, manufacturing, and machinery. There also were dramatic changes in technology, socioeconomics, and culture.

The causes of the Industrial Revolution are still being debated. One theory states that in the 17th century, the borders of Great Britain were better controlled, there was less disease coming into the country from surrounding areas, and more children were living past infancy. All of these conditions led to an increased workforce without enough agricultural work for everyone. Therefore, people began "cottage industries" such as weaving, lace making, and sewing in their homes. Then, in 1700, Jethro Tull invented the seed drill. When farmers used the seed drill, more seeds took root, which led to larger crops, particularly of cotton. As the amount of cotton increased, the demand for products made from cotton also increased. Shortly, the demand for cotton products far exceeded the cottage industries' ability to supply these products. There was a demand for more efficient means of weaving and sewing. According to this theory, then, the Industrial Revolution began in the textile industry to meet the demands of products made from the increased cotton supply.

Another theory cites the expansion of colonial territories, such as America, as the cause of the Industrial Revolution. Expanding territories like America were demanding products from Great Britain. This demand led to the need for more efficient means of production, which then led to the Revolution.

A third theory links the Industrial Revolution to the Scientific Revolution that took place during the 16th century. The Scientific Revolution sparked many inventions, including the steam engine, which made the Industrial Revolution possible.

Although there may be disagreement over the causes of the Industrial Revolution, there certainly is no debate about the many important innovations during this time period, especially in the textile industry. These innovations included the flying shuttle, invented by a watchmaker, which allowed weavers to weave cotton more quickly. Once the

weavers were able to work more quickly, the spinners could not keep up with them. In 1764, James Hargreaves won a contest with his invention, the spinning jenny, which allowed spinners to spin 6–8 threads at once rather than just one thread. Later versions of the spinning jenny could spin as many as 80 threads at once!

In 1769, Richard Arkwright made it possible for spinners to work even faster. He invented the water frame, which used water power to operate spinning wheels, further increasing the speed of the production process. With the water frame, multiple machines could spin at once with just one person overseeing them all; each machine did not need a person operating it. Then, in 1785, Edmund Cartwright patented the power loom, which increased the speed of weaving so the weavers could keep up with the spinners.

Finally, Eli Whitney, who lived in America, invented the cotton gin in 1793. The cotton gin removed seeds from cotton, which was at this point the most time-consuming element of textile production. With this final addition, the process was streamlined and the production of textiles officially became an industry.

THE INDUSTRIAL REVOLUTION

Generalizations

B3 Write at least three generalizations about the Industrial Revolution and how it relates to the modern world.

1. _____

2. _____

3. _____

Classifications

B2 Look at your list from B1. Classify each item on your list into a category. You may not have a "miscellaneous" or "other" category.

_____

_____

_____

_____

_____

_____

Details

B1 List at least 15–20 ways the Industrial Revolution affected the modern world.

_____

_____

_____

_____

_____

_____

_____

_____

_____

_____

Main, Theme, or Concept

C3   Main Idea: What is the main idea of the selection "The Industrial Revolution?"

_____

_____

Write a new title for the selection that better represents its main idea.

_____

_____

Inference

C2   Which of the three theories about the beginning of the Industrial Revolution is best supported by evidence? Explain your answer using details from the text.

_____

_____

_____

_____

_____

_____

_____

Literary Elements

C1   How would you characterize men like Richard Arkwright, Edmund Cartwright, and Eli Whitney? Use details from the text to support your answer.

_____

_____

_____

_____

_____

_____

What's the Chance?

Have you ever tried to determine what your chances were of rolling a 6 with a pair of dice? Or what your chances were of a penny landing on heads versus tails? All of these questions can be answered with a math strategy known as *probability*.

Probability is the measure of how likely an event is to occur based on the number of ways the event could occur and the total number of possible outcomes. Confusing? Let's review some words that are related to probability and then look at an example. Before you can understand probability, you need to know what experiment, outcome, and event mean in relation to it. An *experiment* is a situation that involves chance and leads to outcomes. The result of a single trial is an *outcome*. An *event* is one or more outcomes. OK, now let's look at an example.

Imagine you are rolling a die (that's singular for dice). This is your experiment—you cannot control what number the die will land on, and therefore you are involved in a situation dealing with chance. What is the probability that your die will land on the number 3? Landing on the number 3 would be an outcome or the result of a single trial or roll. How many other possible outcomes are there? Well, you could land on 1, 2, 4, 5, or 6, so there are five other possible outcomes. How many total possible outcomes are there? The total number of possible outcomes is the same as the total of numbers on the die, or six. So, if there is only one outcome that will result in you rolling a 3, and there are six total outcomes, then the chances of you rolling a 3 are 1 in 6 or 1/6. Make sense?

Let's look at another example. Imagine there are four marbles in a bag. One marble is yellow, one is blue, one is green, and one is red. When you pull a marble out of the bag, how many possible outcomes are there? That's right! There are four possible outcomes because there are four different colors. Now, what are your chances of pulling a red marble out of the bag? Only one outcome will lead to a red marble coming out of the bag, so the chances of you drawing a red marble are 1 in 4 or 1/4. The same probability also would apply to the yellow, blue, and green marbles.

Both of these examples are of probability scenarios with equally likely outcomes. When rolling a die, you are equally likely to roll a 4 as you are to roll a 2. When drawing a marble out of the bag, you are equally likely to draw one color as another. Sometimes, though, situations involving probability do not have equally likely outcomes. Probability is considered not equally likely if there is a chance that one outcome will occur more or less frequently than another outcome. For example, imagine you have a bag with six blue candies and three red candies. Are you more likely to draw a blue candy or a red candy? First, let's determine how many total outcomes there are. This number will be the same as the total number of candies, or nine. Now, how many outcomes will result in you pulling a blue candy out of the bag? Six outcomes result in a blue candy, so the probability of you getting a blue candy is 6 out of 9 or 6/9. The chances of you getting a red candy are 3 out of 9 or 3/9 because there are only three red candies. In this example, it is more likely that you will draw a blue candy than a red candy. Therefore, the probability of these events occurring is not equally likely.

WHAT'S THE CHANCE?

Main Idea, Theme, or Concept

C3 Main Idea: What is the main idea of "What's the Chance?" Use evidence from the text to support your answer.

_____

_____

Inference

C2 If P = probability, A = event A, and B = event B, what inferences can you make about the following mathematical sentences?

1. P(A) > P(B)

2. P(A) = P(B)

3. P (A) < P(B)

_____

_____

_____

_____

Literary Elements

C1 If probability were a person, what kind of person would it be? Describe probability. Be sure to include details from the text to support your description.

_____

_____

_____

_____

_____

_____

_____

Creative Synthesis

D3 Write a math word problem that requires the use of probability to solve.

_____

_____

_____

_____

Summarizing

D2 In three sentences or less, describe the differences between equally likely and not equally likely probability.

_____

_____

_____

_____

_____

_____

Paraphrasing

D1 Rewrite the following statement in your own words:

"Probability is the measure of how likely an event is to occur based on the number of ways the event could occur and the total number of possible outcomes."

_____

_____

_____

_____

_____

_____

_____

A World of Resources

Our world is full of many natural resources that people use each and every day. Some examples of natural resources include air, solar energy, aluminum, natural gas, coal, trees, fish, farm animals, and crops. Natural resources can be classified into three different categories: renewable, flow, and nonrenewable.

Renewable natural resources are living resources like fish, deer, trees, and coffee that can grow back or renew themselves with time. In order for a resource to be renewable, the rate of consumption of the resource cannot exceed the amount of time it takes for the resource to replace itself. Metals are an exception to this rule. Metals cannot renew themselves, but they still are considered renewable resources because they can be recycled and reused. Metals, like the aluminum used for soda cans, are not destroyed during the production cycle. Because they are not destroyed, metals are easily melted down and used again and again.

Flow natural resources also are renewable. Unlike renewable resources, though, flow resources do not require time to replenish themselves. Air, water, wind, tides, and solar energy all are examples of flow resources. There is an endless supply of these types of natural resources.

Nonrenewable natural resources are resources that cannot be remade or regrown. Or, if they can be replenished, they cannot be replenished as quickly as the rate of consumption demands. For example, fossil fuels such as coal, natural gas, and petroleum are nonrenewable resources. Fossil fuels can replenish themselves, but the process takes thousands of years. People cannot wait thousands of years for more coal, natural gas, or petroleum. Therefore, these kinds of natural resources are available in limited quantities and considered nonrenewable.

Another way to classify natural resources is by their matter state. Resources can be solid, liquid, or gas. Examples include trees for solid matter, tides for liquid matter, and air for gas matter.

Natural resources also can be classified as organic or inorganic. Organic natural resources are resources that are living or were once living. Organic resources, such as trees, animals, and crops, can live and die. Any resource containing carbon, a byproduct of living organisms, is considered organic. Inorganic resources are resources that are nonliving, such as rocks, water, and air.

Sometimes, we take natural resources for granted because they are everywhere. We forget how important these natural resources are to the way we live our lives. We must all make an effort to appreciate and protect Earth's natural resources.

A WORLD OF RESOURCES

Consequences and Implications

A3   What would be the consequences of using all of the Earth's nonrenewable resources? Give an example to explain your answer.

_____

_____

_____

_____

_____

Cause and Effect

A2   What would be the effect of humans consuming, or using, a renewable resource at a faster rate than it can replenish itself? Use evidence from the text to support your answer.

_____

_____

_____

_____

_____

Sequencing

A1   List the order in which classification of natural resources was discussed in the text.

_____

_____

_____

_____

_____

_____

_____

_____

Generalizations

B3 Write at least three generalizations about natural resources based on your list and your classifications.

_____

_____

_____

_____

_____

_____

_____

_____

Classifications

B2 Using the classifications discussed in the text, classify the natural resources on your list.

_____

_____

_____

_____

_____

_____

_____

Details

B1 List as many natural resources as you can think of in 2 minutes. (List at least 25.)

_____

_____

_____

_____

_____

_____

_____

_____

Routledge
Taylor & Francis Group

www.routledge.com